pickleball faith

Inspiration On And Off The Court

stacy lynn harp. m.s.

contents

Endorsements	ix
Acknowledgments	xi
Foreword	xv
Introduction	xix
Building a Community	1
Pickleball People: The Relationship is the Cure	5
Playing with the Beginner	12
The Beginners Perspective	15
Being Teachable	20
When Conflict Arises	23
Lessons in Obedience	25
You Never Know Who Is in the Ladies Room	30
The Power of Prayer	32
On the Death of Your Friend	35
When a Joke Backfires	39
The Professional Tournament Player Mindset	43
Catching the Ball and Diving for Shots	46
California Pickleball vs. Tennessee	49
People are More Than the Game	52
An Angel in the Locker Room	56
The Cupcake Caregiver	60
Pickleball During a Pandemic	63
Pickleball Faith	69
Afterword	79
Resources	81
About Stacy Lynn Harp	83

Copyright & Attributions

PICKLEBALL FAITH: INSPIRATION ON AND OFF THE COURT

"Scripture taken from the NEW AMERICAN STANDARD BIBLE,

Copyright © 1960, 1962, 1963 1968, 1971, 1972,

1973 1975, 1977, 1995 by The Lockman Foundation

All rights reserved

Used by permission.

http://www.Lockman.org

"What Love Really Means" by JJ Heller and David Heller. Copyright 2010 Butter Lid Publishing/ASCAP (admin by Amplified Administration). All rights reserved. Used by permission.

Thanks to Jay McKey as my creative consultant for the logo and book cover design

Final cover design by Randall K. Harp

Trade Paperback: ISBN: 978-1-7331938-0-1

Ebook: ISBN: 978-1-7331938-1-8

Audio: ISBN: 978-1-7331938-2-5

© 2022, Stacy Lynn Harp, M.S.

All rights reserved: No part of this publication may be reproduced, stored in a retrieval system, or transmitted in any form or by any means —electronic, mechanical, photocopy, recording, or any other —except for brief quotations in printed reviews, without the prior permission of the publisher.

Printed in the United States of America

Created with Vellum

Dedication

Joe Gibbs and Stacy Lynn Harp

Every once in a while there's a person who impacts your life in a special way. For me, that person was Joe Gibbs. Joe and his wife Sharon were the ones who brought pickleball to my local recreation center.

When I first started to play the game, I met Joe and he immediately captured my heart with his wit and winsome personality. He pinched my nose, told me to "shut up" while smiling, and then schooled me on how to make a comeback when you're down nine to zero.

Sadly, Joe died in February of 2019, leaving us way too soon. This book is for you, "Old Geezer". Someday I'll play you on the pickleball courts in heaven.

endorsements

The reason so many people love the exploding sport of pickleball is because of all of the ways that Stacy Lynn describes in this book. She does a great job explaining how faith, community, competitiveness, and relationships make this popular hobby way more than just a game! You will be blessed with the invitation to peer into the sweet heart of Stacy Lynn while joining her on her journey of faith in God and in humanity simply through this crazy sport called pickleball! - **Stephanie Lane, 3 time USA Pickleball National Champion & lover of Jesus!**

Pickleball Faith is for everyone who appreciates spiritual wisdom gleaned from everyday activities. In her "sweet and lovable" style, radio host turned Pickler Stacy Lynn Harp will make you laugh, think, and teach you that the Kitchen isn't where pickleball players go for snacks. - **Dr. Jennifer Fee, Psychologist & TEDx Speaker**

acknowledgments

In my career as a talkshow host, I have read thousands of books and interviewed easily a few thousand people in my career. One of my favorite parts of reading a book is the acknowledgments because it gives me a peek at what happened behind the scenes.

Much like viewing the director's cut to a movie, acknowledgments are given to those who, behind the scenes, offered love and moral support.

With that said, I would like to start by acknowledging the **Lord Jesus Christ**. Obviously nothing would be written from a faith perspective unless I had faith in Someone, and since He is the One who gave me the gift of life and writing, I have to acknowledge Him first. I have written all I have to bring glory to His name.

Second, my dear husband, Bearface, also known as, **Randall K. Harp**. Randall and I have been married since 1992 and he has heard me say more than a million times that I wanted to write, speak, and encourage people in their faith. Equally as important, Randall is my best friend, biggest encourager, lover of my heart, and the best husband a woman could have. A.R.R. forever.

Third, I'd like to thank my friend, **Dr. Jennifer Fee**. Your love, encouragement and friendship warm my heart.

Thank you for paying for those tennis lessons so many years ago and listening to me go on and on forever about pickleball. You were the first to read the manuscript and your encouragement to publish will bless many.

Fourth, I'd like to acknowledge my friends **Dean Weaver**, **David Hart**, **James Richards**, and **Stephanie Lane** who kept a fire burning under me to get this book finished. Your encouragement and friendship mean the world to me and someday, just maybe, I will be able to beat all of you at this game!

Fifth, I'd like to thank my sister in law in law (our siblings are married to each other), **Sandi Frederick**, for not only doing a stellar job editing my manuscript, but also offering so much love and tender encouragement along the way. To you, I say, "Huzzah!"

Next, to all of you in the **Pickleball Community at Longview Recreation Center** in Spring Hill, Tennessee. This book was inspired by all of you. You have enriched my life and made me a better person. I hope you are all blessed and encouraged by the stories I share because of you.

I also want to acknowledge those of you in my **Bible News Radio** community. So many of you have encouraged me along the way and prayed for me. Thank you for all of your love and support of what we do. I know after reading this, you will all play pickleball, won't you?

Lastly, I want to give a special acknowledgment to my all-time mentor and friend, **Lisa E. White**. Without your all time, love, counsel, guidance, and prayers this book would not have been possible. Thank you for teaching me to be real. I love you for always.

foreword

Pickleball Faith is a book with three main themes: faith, pickleball, and relationships. It is an evaluation of faith in Jesus Christ. It will teach you something about the amazing sport of pickleball. It explores the importance of relationships. All of this is done through the eyes and heart of the author: Stacy Lynn Harp.

We are treated to the faith that Stacy has in Jesus Christ. It is her personal relationship with her Lord and Redeemer. It is her Journey into the sport of pickleball. It is the personal relationships Stacy develops while learning and playing pickleball. But don't be fooled into thinking this is a niche story that will have no meaning or appeal to you. The lessons that Stacy explores and the experiences that she shares apply to every situation that you can conjure up. Whether it is being new to your job, facing a geographic move, starting a new relationship, investing time in a hobby, or going on a mission trip—this book can guide you in a positive direction.

Foreword

Stacy is a strong Christian woman, investing more time in her relationship with Jesus than the vast majority of us. Yet she is unafraid to share her failures of faith as well as her growth. This transparency is refreshing, honest and inspirational. She offers us the opportunity to learn and grow while avoiding some of the pitfalls she endured. She demonstrates the joy that can surround us when we act out our faith in the love of Jesus.

The sport of pickleball can be taken literally or metaphorically. You can read this book to be a better pickleball player or you can read it to be a better person in this life. Starting a new endeavor, accepting advice from mentors, learning discernment as to which advice is sound and which is deceiving—all these life lessons are priceless to the person who can listen and apply.

Her relationships with specific people will immediately remind you of certain people in your life. Her experiences will help you understand things which have happened to you and guide you in situations that will occur in the future.

How blessed is the man who finds wisdom, And the man who gains understanding. For her profit is better than the profit of silver, And her gain better than fine gold. Proverbs 3:13-14

Faith is often defined as believing in something you cannot see. The interesting aspect of faith is that you can see it at work in others. We get to see it grow in Stacy and in some of the relationships she encounters. Jesus commanded his followers to love God with all their heart, soul, mind, and strength. He likewise commanded us to love our neighbor as ourself. In Acts 1:8 he says that we will be his witnesses

Foreword

throughout the world. In this book, Stacy Harp is a witness by sharing her relationship with Jesus with every reader. She shares her love for God and for her neighbor. More importantly, she offers every one of us the opportunity and some of the tools to do the same thing. I am a better person for having read this book and I believe you can be too.

David Hart is an Ambassador for Union County, GA. A member of the Board of Directors for USSP (formerly SSIPA), U. S. Senior Pickleball and a Certified Pickleball coach through Professional Pickleball Registry.

introduction

A few years ago I discovered pickleball, or as a friend of mine would say, "pickleball found me" and it literally changed my life. In order to understand the genesis of this book, you need to understand why I have found so much joy in my life when playing pickleball.

The year was 2012 and I had just left Southern California, where I had lived for most of my life. My husband and I felt that God was calling us to move to Tennessee and somehow we ended up in a small town that I had never heard of: Spring Hill, Tennessee, with a population under 30,000. At the time of this writing the town has grown to almost 50,000 people, which is amazing to me.

To make a long story short, after moving and having to deal with culture shock, the one thing that I struggled with was trying to find activities I could do that would involve others away from the local church. I quickly came to notice that, for me, this meant getting involved in some type of exercise class and, for around two years, I enjoyed water aerobics with women often twenty-five to forty years older

Introduction

than I was. I wasn't finding much fulfillment in this and, honestly, was discouraged.

I'm the type of person who loves people and I especially love having fun. My day job is hosting an online live-streaming program called *Bible News Radio* where I get to share the gospel of Jesus Christ with a worldwide audience. I also have had the blessing of meeting and interviewing some of the top authors, speakers, public policy officials, government leaders, and musicians in the world of Christian media. However, even though I love all of that, none of those individuals know me or are in my life on a daily basis.

As a middle-aged woman, married for twenty-nine years, with no children, I've always found it hard to connect with others. The people I've tended to connect with are either much older than I am or often single. I'm not sure why that's been the case, but it is and it started to happen again in the new town in which I found myself. I'm guessing there's something about not having children that attracts singles to you, while at the same time disconnects you from families with children.

As an aside, I have never really had anyone ask me to cook for them, even at a church potluck. I realize that's a random thought, but the truth is that our culture is really family-centered, not couple-centered and really not even single-focused. However, I do believe that there are more things for singles to do than there are for a married couple with no children. At church, family events are usually centered around families *with children*. It isn't until you retire that the church tends to understand that couples have needs outside of their children. I've often felt left out and

Introduction

had a hard time connecting with people as a result. Now back to my other thoughts...

Spring Hill, Tennessee is not Orange County, California. Just as an example, I was used to being able to drive a few minutes for my favorite food, and there were a lot more choices. In Orange County, the culture is not one where everyone will stop to talk to you for an hour in the grocery store, but the friendliness of Spring Hill, that is the case.

So culture shock was a huge issue for me. I felt lonely and discouraged, I honestly felt disillusioned for many reasons, as well. I thought moving to the Bible belt was going to be different than it was. Unfortunately, one of the first things, that happened to us was that we were taken advantage of by a local contractor who worked on our house. Something I just didn't expect or see coming. And when the person who referred that contractor to me didn't step in to help, I just felt all the more disillusioned with our move to the Bible Belt, because I had never experienced that type of service in California. But God had a blessing for me in Spring Hill that I didn't see originally.

With that background, one day I was at the local Parks and Recreation Center and was walking on the upper floor track when I happened to note that there were some people playing a game that looked like tennis. I had no idea what it was, but it grabbed my attention and I made my way down to the bottom floor so I could see what it was.

After thinking about this for a few minutes, I made my way to the front desk to inquire what this new sport was. They told me it was *pickleball*. Then they said that if I wanted to play, all I had to do was go and join the game.

Introduction

I was shocked and honestly excited. I remember making my way back to the court and asking some questions about how to play. To my absolute joy, they told me to pick a paddle and write my name on a piece of paper, and then wait until I was called.

And that is where this story really begins.

building a community
. . .

If you are human—and clearly you are because you're reading this book—then you know that belonging is everything.

We live in a world today that I refer to as the most "connected" and yet truly "disconnected" world. We have cell phones, computers, and social media that were designed to make our lives easier and to help us "connect" more, yet the research shows that these things have done exactly the opposite.

The first thing that happened to me when I stepped out to learn the game of pickleball was that I started to connect again with some real people. It was exciting, refreshing, and let's just say it, very cool!

I have played tennis since high school, but the last time I had done so before that day in 2016 was in 2009, when I won first place in a mental health charity tournament. So, I was familiar with how to play a racket sport, but quickly found out that the rules in pickleball were *not* the same as in tennis.

In another aside: there are many of us "retired" tennis players that have gone to pickleball and we understand the adjustments that need to be made.

I was welcomed in by the men that were there that first day at the Rec Center. I'd say there was about an eight-to-one ratio of men to women; we were outnumbered. I quickly found that some of these men loved poaching my shots and telling me what to do with every move. If I missed a shot, they pointed it out. If I went into the kitchen, they would let me know. If I didn't run up to the line fast enough, they told me. And if you're reading this and are a seasoned pickleball player, I bet you're laughing right now because all of that is so common.

In fact, I can't ever remember being instructed that much while playing tennis. However, pickleball is not tennis. We all know that.

And this my dear reader friend, is where the community starts.

The game of pickleball is actually about *community*. As with many sports, communities are built around a chosen sport, but honestly, with pickleball it really goes deeper. That's why I'm writing this book. I want you to see how pickleball has not only increased my faith in humanity again, but also how, as a Christian, I have seen my faith worked out in and through the community that God has built here in my local town of Spring Hill, Tennessee.

What makes a community? This is one question that I think needs to be addressed. For the purpose of this book, I am defining a community as the group of people who play pickleball together, have lunch together, go to other events together and, in short, just being together.

I remember telling my husband that I was more connected to this community of pickleball players than I have ever been in any of the churches I've attended in the past. In fact, when I attended church on Sunday morning and Sunday night and also on Wednesday and even in a midweek Bible study, I didn't spend as much time with those friends as I have with my pickleball friends.

This is vital to understand because I generally play around twelve hours of pickleball a week. Sometimes it's a little bit more and other times a little bit less. The point is that when I play four days a week, I made a commitment to stay for a few hours at a time. You would be amazed at how much you can bond with people while you're waiting for your next game.

Also, it is interesting to note that when you are actively engaged in a physical activity, as opposed to simply sitting in a church pew listening to a preacher, there is more room to grow as a person. I am going to share with you some personalities that I've encountered that have stretched me and grown me in my faith.

But first, let me be sure to share with you that everything I am going to share is designed with the intent and purpose to encourage. My goal has always been to uplift people. To make people feel loved and welcomed. To make people laugh and to believe in others. I spent over thirteen years in college to earn my Masters of Science degree in clinical psychology and I practiced as a marriage and family therapist for many years, so I love helping others.

But here is something vital to know, not everyone wants help and not everyone is teachable. This book is about how God has taught me things. How to grow in patience and understanding. How to trust people again. How to work together towards a common goal. How to work as a team. How to pick myself up after falling, both literally and figuratively, and most important, how to stay and belong when it can be tough.

I am convinced that most people are lonely. If you look at research and data your eyes may glaze over, because data is boring to the average person, but the reality is that most people are lonely. I think the rise in suicide rates and the breakdown in the family are evidence of that. That is why having a community is so important.

If you listen or watch my show, *Bible News Radio*, then you know that I took care of my elderly father. He was born in 1928 and lived a very long life before passing in 2021. I moved him into an assisted living community after the death of his fourth wife because I knew I wasn't able to take care of him well enough, and because I knew living in a community would be far better for his emotional health. People who put together these assisted living places understand this.

So in the following chapters we will look at community and see how my first clinical supervisor shared with me how "The relationship is the cure".

pickleball people: the relationship is the cure
. . .

When I was doing my clinical supervision as a therapist, my first clinical supervisor, Dr. Paul Alexander, would always end our supervision sessions with the phrase, "The relationship is the cure." I have no idea if he coined that expression or not, but in all of the things I've ever learned from my training in working with people, that phrase has been forever ingrained in my mind.

On the pickleball court you are developing relationships with people whether you like it or not. I say that in jest, in part, because you can tell (well, I should say, I can tell) when a person has had difficulty in their relationships. I actually love talking to people and just listen to what they say. I actually *listen* to what they say, and how they say it. In fact, if you want to get a good indicator of someone's self-talk, then play pickleball, because you'll hear that self-talk come out of their mouth every time they miss a shot or they feel like they've done something wrong.

Maybe it's because I'm sensitive to my surroundings and by nature an empath, but I really *feel* what people say. I easily feel other's emotion, both good and bad. So when you play pickleball with a partner, you can *hear* what they think. Some people will attack themselves constantly. Others will attack you or criticize you. In some cases they may "instruct" you—not because you asked them to, but because they have a need to. In essence what I see by that is what *they* need or believe they need.

I believe that most people don't want to let their pickleball partners down. Most of us. There may be a few people who don't care, but ultimately when you're playing a paddle sport, you're more of an individualistic person anyway and you're usually a leader. I say *usually* because people who play sports—like swimming or golf—that are more focused on *individual* than *team* performance, tend to be more individual.

When you take these individualists and you put them in a game *with* someone, you're going to see how they act. Just as an aside and fun-fact, when I surveyed my friends most of them are first borns and/or only children. I wasn't surprised by this. It made sense to me because that's the type of sport pickleball is.

But if we want to get back to the phrase, "The relationship is the cure", then we have to look at how we talk to ourselves on the court and how our partner talks to us.

I always try to encourage my partner. I don't criticize because I don't like being criticized. I don't thrive on judgment. I don't thrive when people tell me what I'm doing wrong. I thrive on being told what I did right. Most people, if they are honest, will tell you that they do better when they are encouraged.

In fact, just as an aside, I recently had a friend on my show who told me about a famous "rice experiment". The researcher, a Japanese scientist named Dr. Masaru Emoto, did this experiment and actually discovered something amazing. He wanted to test the power of our words. Some people say "intention". I don't care for that phraseology, so for my example here, I'm going to say power. The Bible instructs us all over the book of Proverbs about how to use our words. One famous scripture says, "As a man thinks in his heart, so is he." (Proverbs 23:7) and the reality is, that it's true!

So in the rice experiment, what Dr. Emoto did was boil some white rice and then sterilized three jars. After he did that, he put an equal amount of rice in each jar and then labeled the jars *Love*, *Hate*, and *Ignore*. He then spoke to each rice jar in words that matched the label. My friend showed me the results of her experiment doing the same thing and it was amazing. In fact, you can go to You Tube and look up numerous examples and see how people have replicated Dr. Emoto's study.

The results of were amazing. When loving words were spoken to the rice, the rice stayed white. When hateful words were spoken, the rice turned an ugly black and when the ignored rice was ignored, it was even blacker.

Dr. Emoto did other research, talking to water and then freezing it. After examination under a microscope, he noted that the words of hate caused jagged edges and the loving words caused beautiful creations. I realize this sounds crazy, but honestly, it's been done, it's been replicated and there is genuinely something about the power of our words.

So in our relationships, if the "relationship is the cure", then we want to be kind and speak kindly to our partners. We can only do this the best way if we have learned to speak nicely to ourselves, too.

What I have learned playing pickleball with my friends is that God has had to stretch me concerning my own thoughts and behavior. I want to be my best but it's more important to me to encourage others. When I miss a shot, I may say, "Dang it! or Grr," or "Maybe next time." What I observed other better players do is say to the person who hit the shot that they missed, "Great shot!" - And that builds *up* the relationship. It takes the focus off of the perceived failure and puts it back on to the accomplishment.

Look at it this way:

Failure or error = sickness; success and accomplishment = cure.

So, if the relationship is the cure, then focusing on the successes and the accomplishments is what we want. The best way to do this is by realizing what your self-talk is first. Focus on what *you* say to *yourself* and learn to identify where you need growth and then you'll be able to offer not only encouragement to yourself, but also to your partners.

One of my favorite scriptures in the whole Bible is Ephesians 4:29. In the New American Standard Version of the Bible, this is how this verse is translated, "Let no unwholesome word proceed from your mouth, but only such a word as is good for edification according to the need of the moment, so that it will give grace to those who hear."

Let's examine this verse and see what we can learn. The first thing we are told is to let no unwholesome word proceed from our mouths. The word unwholesome literally means, in the Greek, rotten. It also means worthless (literally and morally) and also bad or corrupt and putrid. *Putrid* is a word that gets your attention, doesn't it? (*Putrid* reminds me of the smell of rotten eggs.) The point is that according to the Bible, *no* unwholesome, rotten, putrid, bad, corrupt words should come out of our mouths. Why? Well, this verse goes on to tell us. It's ultimately because those words do not give grace to the hearer.

What is *grace* you may be wondering? Well, the simple, biblical definition of grace is that which affords joy, pleasure, delight, sweetness, charm, loveliness: "grace of speech". Isn't that cool?

Let's go back to the verse. The next part says that we should only say words that are good for edification, according to the need of the moment. I love this! Edification is one of my favorite words. Here's what the word means from the Greek. It comes from the word *oikodomé*, pronounced oy-kod-om-ay, which means building, or edifying. Simply put, it means to build up. In this context, it means to build others up with your words.

We are instructed to use words that build up others and offer them joy, pleasure, delight, sweetness, charm, and loveliness. In other words, it makes that person feel good! But don't miss the other part of the phrase, "according to the need of the moment". What moment are we talking about in pickleball? Well, the moment you are on the court playing, but also those moments when you are off the court talking and sharing.

Stacy Lynn Harp. M.S.

Here's another thing I recently discovered about this verse: *giving grace to those who hear*. I used to think that meant that your words should give grace to those who are listening to you. When I really stopped to think about this, though, I came to realize that my own words also have the power to give grace to myself.

I touched on that a little bit earlier. If what we can speak out loud to a bowl of rice can impact that rice by changing its color, then how much more can it actually impact us and our own health? Our words have the power to heal. Life and death are in the power of the tongue, and those who love it will eat its fruit. (Proverbs 18:21) We have the power to build up others or to tear them down. We must be wise in what we choose.

There's also an interesting correlation that I read about in the book *The Slight Edge* by Jeff Olson. Olson writes about some of the research done by Dr. Marty Seligman concerning positive psychology and the study of how people become happy. In fact, it was only about twenty years ago that positive psychology became an area of study. This study of how people are happy is very interesting because there was a study done that showed an interesting correlation between bad words written on Twitter and heart disease. Jeff Olson writes…

"The study had analyzed some 40,000 words in over 80 million tweets, and when the results were overlaid with a county-by-county analysis of heart attacks, it was a nearly exact correlation.

What kind of language patterns were so predictive of illness? Overall, they were expressions of anger, hostility, and aggression, as well as disengagement and lack of social support, including,

"Mad, alone, annoying, can't, mood, bored, tired" —a slew of words that I can't repeat here.

He next showed charts displaying the correlation of a *positive* attitude and *lower* risk of heart attacks, and they were just as dramatic. The slide of words that correlated with low incidence of atherosclerotic disease included: "morning, fabulous, helpful, share, running, forward, great, interesting, lunch, discussion, seems." - *The Slight Edge*, **page 100**

Now let's talk about playing with beginners in our next chapter.

playing with the beginner

. . .

One purpose of this book is to tell you honest stories about how God has used pickleball to build me up in my faith. Here are some honest truth bombs.

When I was a beginner, I had some very nice people take me in and teach me the game. I picked it up relatively quickly because of my tennis background. I am no expert by any means, and maybe on a super good day will rate around a 3.5 player. It is subjective, but I'd say that right now, on average, that's about my level. But when you're playing with beginners, you're not going to be playing a fast game.

In the years I've been playing pickleball, I'd have to say that most of the growth in my faith walk has occurred when playing with beginners. This chapter is about sharing how God has shown me my own arrogance and pride (though I hate to admit it) and how I have had to return to my roots to slow down and learn.

One of the things that actually annoys me is that not all players will play with beginners. In fact, I've seen a ton of shunning on the pickleball courts because many of the better players do not want anything to mess with their game of pickleball. They are not about the relationship being the cure. They want to play and they want to play at their level. I get that and I respect it. If your full purpose in playing pickleball is to be a professional and play tournaments all of the time, that's fine. If you want to help a newbie out and you want to be an encourager, then play with beginners.

There's a phrase I've seen numerous times: "All experts were once beginners." Yeah, they were. I've been interviewing people professionally now for over seventeen years and when I started interviewing others I just took the natural gift that God gave me and ran with it. However, I studied great communicators and literally took notes on what I heard them do. It's the same way with pickleball. In order for a beginner to become better and to become the expert, someone has to teach them.

I remember one day when my friend JR was teaching a beginner and I was being super selfish inside my heart. I was on the opposing team and I was waiting for JR between shots as he instructed the newbie. He was taking what felt like two or three minutes between serves and I eventually got so mad at him that I quit the game. I intentionally missed the final shots and then I walked off the court. I was being a snot and a brat. A forty-something, middle-aged woman, acting like a brat because she had to WAIT and didn't like it.

As I write this, I'm laughing out loud, not because it's really *funny* but because I'm just being honest. That day, playing with beginners wasn't fun for me. But my friend JR is a gem. He's one of the most patient men I have ever met. He's kind, he's a smiling man, and he has taught me more about relationships than 3,000 hours of clinical internship. He cares about the beginner because he sees the future.

Another time I was sitting on the sidelines waiting to play another game with beginners, and I was there because I was asked to come and help. I didn't mind helping, but I made the mistake of verbalizing to the newbie that I would "play down" for them so that they could hit the ball back. I unintentionally insulted that person and they snapped back at me, "I don't want you to play down for me, how am I going to get better if you 'play down?'" Then they got up and moved their paddle so I didn't have to play with them.

I remember feeling like crap. I later apologized to that player because I realized that my attitude was one of superiority instead of humility. Instead of saying, "I will play down to help you" I could have not said anything or I could have said to them, "What would *you* like to work on as far as your game goes? What would you like to learn?"

I believe if you're a good teacher then your *students* will teach *you* and you'll be better off for it. Remember, the relationship is the cure. Being a showy know-it-all helps no one.

the beginners perspective

. . .

Have you ever considered that you have been a beginner in something? I think if they are honest, most people don't think that way. Especially as adults, because we're *adults*. We already know how to read and write and we can drive a car, we play whatever sports we like and we've got some years under our belts. No one is forcing us to really learn anything new, unless you are in a job that calls for it. As a clinically trained therapist, if I were still practicing, I would be required by law to complete a certain number of continuing education units. However, most jobs don't really demand that, so when someone decides that they are going to learn something new, it's not under *compulsion*, but rather *intention*.

A very good friend of mine has trained me to remember that people are always a product of their own environment and that I need to remember their perspective in the situation. When you're playing with a beginner in pickleball, you're going to be playing with someone who is trying to learn something new, and everyone learns new things in their own way.

A perfect illustration of this is what happened at a game I played recently.

I had not played for about a week and when I arrived at the courts, there weren't many people there. Since I had been sick and dealing with pretty severe allergies, I opted to play with everyone. I don't always, because there are days I want to play at my level. However, that day there were some beginners who wanted to play and the more advanced players *didn't* want to play with the beginners. So, JR and I both took one of the beginners and played a game.

One was an older lady who told me that she had played tennis before, but she was new at this game. The other beginner was a boy who had to be about eleven years old. He was quite new and usually hung out with adults. I'm not sure if he's an only child or what his situation was, but he was very interested in pickleball and so we took the time to play with him. I figure anytime a child wants to be active instead of sitting at a computer playing a game, I'll help them out.

Before the game, JR made a point to say that another friend was waiting for him so he could go to lunch, so I understood that was going to be his last game and yet, in his typical wonderful fashion, JR didn't speed up the game. In fact, it ended up being quite a long game of about 30 minutes.

Why?

We were both trying to teach and remember to consider the perspective of the two beginners.

Pickleball Faith

The boy was having a great time. I could tell that all he wanted to do was play and he honestly didn't care how long it took. He wasn't doing anything else. He had the attention of three adults who were investing time in him and were helping him learn a new game. When I asked him how he would like me to serve the ball to him—harder or soft—he yelled back, "I don't care, just serve the ball!" So I did. My serves were both hard and soft. He hit the ball as if it were a baseball being pitched. It went out of bounds and we all laughed.

The older lady's perspective was very different. She was happy to be playing but wasn't confident about anything that she did. She had a hard time serving the ball into the court and she didn't pay attention when the ball was served to her. She actually said that she didn't realize that we were both trying to help her learn. But she hung in there and played the whole game, and afterwards asked if we would all play again. She wanted to continue to learn.

Most of us don't make a conscious choice to think about others' perspectives, unless they've been put in a circumstance that required them to learn empathy or compassion. When it comes to sports, empathy and compassion aren't generally the first terms that come to mind. Let's face it, when we think of sports, we think of competition, fun, and angry parents and coaches who want their kids to win. (I'm only slightly kidding about that last line.)

Another point I want to make regarding playing with beginners is that a person may not be an actual *beginner*, but they may be an older person who has *slowed down* in life. I had to learn to slow down a lot due to taking care of my elderly father.

One day I was feeling frustrated again—yeah I, admit it—because I was playing with a lady that had played tennis for years and yet for some reason on that particular day she wasn't playing well. I couldn't figure out why. But I thought, *Well, maybe she's having an off day*. Then a short time later I decide to ask my friends this question:

"What is one thing that you've survived that you thought you were never going to be able to get through?"

This was such an open-ended question that I had no idea what the answers would be, but that day I asked the lady I was playing with that question. She said, and I quote, "Learning to walk again…twice."

BET YOU WEREN'T EXPECTING that were you? Well, neither was I. I asked her what had happened, and she shared with me that when she was a child she got run over by a truck, and then when she was older she fell off a horse. Both times she had to learn to walk again and yet there she was playing pickleball! (Incidentally, her husband was also in an accident and lost his hand and part of one arm, so he plays with one hand. He inspires me, too!)

Remember I told you how I was feeling about how she was playing that day? Well, my perspective about playing with her completely changed, knowing that she had to learn to walk twice. Instead of feeling frustrated, I was inspired!

Life is all about perspective. It's about relationships and how our relationships cure us of our own self-centeredness. Consider that the next time you're playing pickleball and are asked to play with someone you may not normally play with. What is that beginner's perspective? What is their backstory? You may be surprised at the miracle you're getting the opportunity to experience.

being teachable
. . .

I hope that last chapter encouraged you to think differently about playing with someone you may not have considered playing before, and I hope this chapter shows you that there's a difference between being *teachable* and being *taught*.

Years ago, a young arrogant man attended junior college to work toward earning his Associates Degree. He was in a writing class and the professor graded him down on some of his work. The student felt as if he knew better than the professor and ultimately got so offended that he quit college, never to return. That's being unteachable and is never good for anyone involved.

My father, who was a veteran of the Korean War, often told me the story of how he was commanding a platoon of soldiers, giving them orders to be very careful while walking through the minefields because if they stepped on a live mine, they could be killed. He relayed this story to me often. That was in part due to his dementia, but also because one of the men under his command didn't heed and obey orders and as a result lost his life when he stepped on a mine. That soldier wasn't teachable, and it cost him his life.

I doubt that not heeding the advice of your pickleball instructor or another player would cost you your life, but the point is that if you're teachable then you will learn new and better ways to play the game. If you're someone who isn't teachable, you eventually will not have many people who want to play with you and you're not going to get any better at the game. Sadly, I know of one man this has happened to and it really didn't have to if he could just change his attitude.

As we've already established, pickleball is a game but it's also about how to get along with others. How to be in relationships that will help you grow.

My mentor reminded me of the movie *Karate Kid*, and the "wax on, wax off" scenes. If you saw the movie then you'll recall that the Kid—Daniel—wasn't all that happy with all of the chores he was doing for Mr. Miyagi, but in the end those little chores helped develop him into becoming a karate champion.

One day when I was first beginning to learn pickleball, there was a lady that was visiting and she joined me in a game. I knew almost immediately that she had played and won many tournaments; that much was clear from her playing and her confidence. I was feeling frustrated because at that time several men at the Rec Center were poaching shots from me. (Sorry guys, but in all of my playing I've never had a female partner poach my shot.) Anyway, it was bothering me and I told this tournament winner and I'll never forget what she said. "Stand your ground and don't move when they try to poach you and they will eventually stop it." Then she said that she thought it was innate for men to simply want to help their female counterparts.

I'm not sure of that assessment, but I will tell you that it was tough for me *not* to move when I thought I was going to get hit when I could see my partner coming after my shot. Despite my fear, however, I started to stand my ground and take those shots. That instructor—the proven champion—was right—they all backed off.

Being teachable means that you are open to change. It means that you listen and then do. Recently, I polled my Facebook audience and asked them this: "Are you a hearer or a doer?" Some people answered the question with "Both", but most people actually picked *one* of the choices. What was interesting to me, and not at all surprising, was that those who admitted they are mostly hearers are people who are largely stuck in life, they tend to be more depressed than others and they generally have a pessimistic outlook on life. Being a hearer is useless unless you do something with what you hear. In the small epistle of James, in the Bible, we see the following verses:

"But prove yourselves doers of the word, and not merely hearers who delude themselves. For if anyone is a hearer of the word and not a doer, he is like a man who looks at his natural face in a mirror for once he has looked at himself and gone away, he has immediately forgotten what kind of person he was." (James 1:23-24)

I have always loved these verses because they give a vivid picture of someone who *hears* but doesn't *do*. If you want to improve your pickleball game or your relationships in life, learn to listen to others who can instruct you. Be teachable and then do what they tell you to. You'll grow and improve. I promise.

when conflict arises
. . .

Whatever doesn't break you, makes you stronger. It's an old saying, and I like it, but I like what my husband says better. "Blessed are the flexible for they shall bend and not snap." In the world of relationships, and especially when you're playing with various temperaments and personality types on the pickleball court, it is good to remember this.

Sometimes a conflict is simple. Someone may call a ball out, when in fact the ball was in. Most of us don't have eagle vision so we can't see the ball perfectly, which is why we defer to the other side to be honest and make the correct call. However, there are times when bad calls are made and, depending on whom you're playing with, this may determine if there will be some conflict.

Unfortunately, where there are people, there is conflict. I've seen men almost punch one another over whose turn it was to get the next open court. I've heard some vulgar language from a few men—who frankly should know better—because they got offended that something didn't go their way. I've played with men who have insulted me personally because they wanted to play a more competitive game and yet because I was in it, they decided to tell me what to do every play of the game. Dealing with these problematic personality types is draining; there are days when you just have to realize some people make it difficult for anyone to want to play with them as they attempt to take over the courts and have it all their way.

My hope in writing so candidly about this is that if this is going on where you are playing that you just consider the source and move on. Life is too short to deal with players who should know better. Eventually they will get a clue, and either everyone will stop playing with them or they will learn to get along and play cooperatively.

What I have learned from pickleball bullies is that they are self-centered. They don't care about how they treat others, they only care about when they get to play and with whom they want to play.

I've seen some of these bullies rearrange paddles so that they throw out people they consider less worthy than the best to play with. I've seen these bullies act like they are the best players while making simple mistakes themselves. They tend to blame their partners for their errors and don't take any personal responsibility for their actions. It's actually very sad. They don't get that the relationship is the cure.

So how do you deal with conflict on the court? You deal with it the way you deal with conflict in your every day life. Some people confront it head on. Others are avoidant. Some people are peacemakers. I've personally used all three tactics because I know people and ultimately I have to take care of myself.

lessons in obedience
. . .

God has taught me a lot through pickleball. Sometimes when I stop and think about all the things He has taught me, I am actually humored. Maybe it's because I'm getting older, but I seem to find lessons in many things.

When I first started playing pickleball, there were a group of people there that worked at Mars. Mars happens to manufacture——the product that my dogs and millions of others love: Greenies! My friend who worked at Mars was one of their food engineers and he often brought pet treats in order to figure out what was in them so that they could compete and make their Mars products better. One day, out of the blue, he brought me about ten bags of Greenies. I was delighted. I own two purebred Bichon Frise's who love Greenies, but I rarely buy them because they are expensive and I live on a tight budget. I don't have money for expensive dog treats. I thanked my friend and came home blessed.

I share this because for well over a year this man and his wife provided me with these awesome pet treats. They gave them to me out of the kindness of their hearts because it didn't cost them anything and they knew my dogs loved them. I saw this as a blessing from God.

Then one day it happened. Someone came to me and asked if I would donate a few dollars to a fund that some of the players were putting together for people back in the Philippines. They had brought some pies and were trying to sell them so that they could raise money to buy pickleball paddles and nets and balls for the people in the Philippines. And here comes a truth bomb—that particular day I was full of self-pity and really down on people, and bummed out because I felt that no one donated or cared about the work I did for my show. I promptly told the person who asked for a donation, and I quote, "No. I don't have the money and I rely on people donating to me."

My friend responded, "Anything would help, can you donate one dollar?"

"No," I said, and she walked away a little sad.

While I was playing a game a short while later, the Lord spoke to me and said, "You know that twenty dollar bill you have in your car so you can go out to lunch with some of these folks later?"

I answered silently, "Yes, I'm aware of it."

The Lord said, "I want you to give it to them for the Philippines."

In all honesty, I was unhappy about that. I was actually annoyed and started to argue with the Lord in my head.

"But God, come on. You know how much money I make." Etc.

And as I was getting ready to serve the ball, I said, "Fine . . . after this game is over I will go to my car and I will get the twenty dollars and give it to her because You said so." The game ended and a few people wanted me to keep playing, but I said, "I can't, I have to go to my car first to get something."

As I was walking to my car the Lord asked me a question. "How much do you think those Greenies that you've been given this past year would have cost if you were to have bought them?"

I said, "Well, well over a hundred dollars, at least. Probably more." And then I got the point and I started to laugh.

I was like, "Okay, I get it, Lord. I'm going to get the money and give it to my friend, I'll apologize to her for being selfish and repent."

Now if you happen to not be a Christian and you're reading this story, all of this may sound crazy, but that's okay. My faith in Jesus Christ is a personal relationship and I'm just sharing with you an actual conversation I had with Him and what happened.

I got the twenty dollar bill and promptly and obediently went straight for my friend on the courts and gave it to her . I told her I was sorry and that the Lord had just disciplined me and told me to apologize to her for being selfish.

Then I walked away.

Two things happened there. First, my friend was shocked that I would do what I just did, especially based on what I had very rudely said to her before. Second, I was reminded of how much God had given me despite how selfish I was. Everyone at pickleball knew of my faith and that I host *Bible News Radio*. What a *great* witness for Christ I had turned out to be that day. *Eventually*.

But here's the thing, when you're honest, real, and transparent, people get it. In fact, it was probably a month or so later that this friend of mine who had asked for the donations actually was having a bad day and snapped at me on the court. Later she apologized to everyone in our Spring Hill Pickleball group. And of course, we all forgave her.

A short time after this event took place, God ended up blessing me financially through an unexpected source. Even as I type this I am smiling because I know that even despite my sinful fleshly self, God is a good God and He loves me. He loves you too, just in case you forgot. The thing about following Jesus is that He knows our frame and that we are "but dust". He understands that we are going to fall and that we are going to get back up. He's a good parent who genuinely loves us and He gives us comfort even if He has to discipline us. He also rewards our obedience.

Another occasion the Lord had to discipline me was when I felt hurt over someone that I was trying to bless by playing with them, when no one else really liked to. She was an older Christian lady who said something that I felt offended by and it really stuck into my heart. Then I noticed that *she* was acting hurt and—to make a long story short—she actually confronted me as a Christian and said, "Hey we need to talk about what's bothering you." To be honest, I didn't feel like it and I didn't want to. But I did.

After a short time we both expressed our hurt feelings and hugged and it was dealt with. I don't think she knows how much that impacted me. It hit powerfully because I felt misunderstood and under-appreciated while in reality she really did appreciate me. Our wires just got crossed. After that, I really enjoyed playing with her because she's inspiring to me. Here's a woman who conquered cancer and keeps on moving. By comparison, I'm a young twit. I mean that in a good way.

This all goes back to *the relationship being the cure*. I have a few more stories to share, but first, I need to share the bathroom story. Keep reading.

you never know who is in the ladies room

. . .

Before I share this story, my husband tells me that this would *never* happen with men. He's probably right.

One day I was taking a break from playing and had to visit the ladies bathroom. I was at the sink, washing my hands, and started talking to the other lady who was washing *her* hands. We started chatting about our exercise and she told me she was about to walk on the treadmill. I told her I found that boring and she agreed, so I invited her to play pickleball with me instead.

She asked, "What's pickleball?" and that was where it started. I told her it was like tennis, but on a smaller court, and invited her to come play with us.

She said, "Okay," and the rest is history.

I had the opportunity to teach her the game and, in the following months, watched her excel and eventually enter and *win* a few tournaments. It was really cool and I couldn't have been more proud.

Did I tell you who the woman was? No, but I will. It happened to be one of our city's Aldermen. In other states, the position would be called a City Councilwoman. I had no idea, when we met.

And you may be wondering *why* I'm sharing this story. I met a public official in a public bathroom. *Who cares?* I do. This was actually just a fun story and I love it because it never would have happened when I lived in a big city in California. Sometimes God connects you to people, often in strange places, and for nothing except to be a blessing to you all.

My husband is right—all of that likely would not have happened between men, but women are different. I hope it made you smile.

As an addendum: As this woman was an Alderman, and then Vice Mayor of our city, she actually lobbied for *more pickleball courts* because the sport has become so popular here in recent years.

That is the beauty of pickleball!

the power of prayer
. . .

This next story is by far one of the coolest things I've seen God do at pickleball. But again, it's about my lack of faith and eventual obedience to what He wanted me to do.

I play with a lot of people who are between 20 and 30 years older than I. There's one couple whom I instantly fell in love with when I started to play, because I just resonated with them: Joe and Sharon. Joe was a retired entrepreneur and he liked to pinch my nose and tell me to, "Shut up," just because. He did it all in fun and I love it—except for the nose part, which I told him and he stopped. He was stronger than my nose preferred.

They had to leave for a while and when they finally returned, Sharon wasn't doing well. She came to pickleball with Joe, but she was using a walker and had lost a lot of weight. She was concerned because the doctors had no idea what was wrong. I told her that I would pray for her.

A few weeks went by and Sharon got worse. I had a guest on my show who talked about the power of prayer and God's will for us to be healed. My guest encouraged me to pray *with* her, not just *for* her. I told her I had no clue if Sharon was a Christian, and I was scared to initiate a prayer time with her, but I agreed I would try.

To make a long story short, the day finally came when Sharon came back to pickleball. Because I had promised my guest and God, I hesitantly went up to her and asked, "Hey, how ya feeling?"

Sharon replied, "Not doing so well," and went on to explain all of her ailments and how she felt discouraged.

I felt her pain because I really loved this woman and I loved Joe and I hated to see them both so sad. So, with a bit of fear and trepidation, I said to her, "I believe that God wants us well. He tells us that He has come to heal us. Do you mind if I pray for you right now?"

Sharon responded, "Oh no, honey . . . I'll take all the prayer I can get." Relieved, but a still a little scared, I put my arm around her and bowed my head and prayed the little prayer of faith that I had for her healing. Keep in mind there were a ton of people playing pickleball and sitting around us, so it wasn't like the prayer was said in a closed room.

I remember after I left that day, saying to the Lord, "I hope you heal her. I did what You said." Oh, "me of little faith".

The next week, Joe came up to me and gave me a hug and a big smile. This was out of the ordinary, because usually he walked by and told me to "Shut up" in the teasing way he had with me. I asked him what happened and he said,

"Sharon's doing great. It's been a week now and she's getting better and doesn't need her walker anymore."

I asked, "Did she tell you I prayed for her?"

"Yes," he said. "keep it up, and thank you."

As I write this, I have tears in my eyes because God is good. Even if God had not healed Sharon of her situation, He would still be good. But this was a story of my faith or lack of it, and God coming through and touching the lives of others.

Though Joe has since died and Sharon was widowed, I still hold the experience close in my "pickleball faith".

on the death of your friend
. . .

I have to be honest and share here that this book was delayed, in part, because I had been putting off writing about the unexpected death of my friend Joe. Back in February of 2019, four of my friends died and the death that shocked me the most was Joe's.

It happened during an optimistic time in my life. I had designed a t-shirt for our local pickleball community. I had bought a couple of t-shirts for Joe and Sharon—who had gone down to Florida for the winter—and was looking forward to surprising them with the shirts when they returned home.

Well, unbeknownst to me, Joe had fallen seriously ill while they were in Florida. I had not seen him in months and then one day out of the blue, someone posted in our small Facebook community that Joe had died.

I was devastated. I was shocked and overwhelmed. Over a period of a few days, everyone in the group online was notified. I went to our local courts to play pickleball and I had the blessing of telling my other friends about what had happened to Joe. (I wept even as I typed this because the feelings were still raw.)

There is something special, though, that took place during that time that made a profound impact upon me: A community of competitive people came together during a time of grief. Many people generally hide their grief during such times, but the people I'd grown to genuinely care for showed their love and grief among one another.

I remember the reactions of some of the men in particular. One friend kept saying, "Oh no, no, no!" when he heard the news. Another friend started to weep when he heard the news. Probably a hundred hugs were given and the community came together for Joe's funeral.

Before the funeral, a friend of mine called and suggested that the shirts that I bought for Joe and Sharon be signed and brought to the services. I thought that this was a great idea, so I took a few weeks to gather the signatures and presented the shirts to Sharon on the day of Joe's memorial service, alongside a love offering that the community had also taken up for her.

Sharon was touched and thanked me a few months later when she came back to visit the pickleball courts. In fact, that day was also super emotional for everyone because she had written a thank you card to everyone. My friend JR, to whom she had given the card, brought her to the middle of the courts while everyone was there. Sharon was weeping and everyone stopped their games to hear what she said. I cried with her, we all hugged, and the community grew stronger.

Just as that gathering was a testimony, so was Joe's memorial service a testimony to what a great guy he was. Two of our friends drove all day from *Florida* to attend the service. It was an amazing display of love and compassion.

I can't explain why I loved Joe so much, and still do, but I can tell you that he will forever have a piece of my heart. He was a very kind man, had a great sense of humor, loved his wife, his family, his friends, and he loved pickleball. It's because of him and Sharon that pickleball came to be where it is in my city. His work changed my life and I will forever be grateful. I will forever be grateful to the Lord for giving me a friend like Joe and I will forever be grateful for the last time I saw him.

Let me tell you about that.

The community center where we play pickleball had decided to do a party for all of us. We joined together, had a potluck, and Joe and Sharon were there. I walked around the room taking pictures of everyone, but when it came to taking a picture of Joe, I almost didn't do it. I'm not sure why I hesitated but I did eventually go up to him and ask if I could take a picture with him. He agreed and I will forever treasure it. That is the picture you see in the Dedication section of this book.

In fact, the conversation around this picture is funny to me because we were joking about him dying on the pickleball court and the police coming and having to put tape around his body. We joked that if he died, then we would have to have the pickleball courts named after him. We both had a warped sense of humor.

Little did I know that less than six months later he would be gone, and I'd be writing these words and remembering him in this way. It just goes to show you that you never know when it will be the last time you see someone. Always remember that. Tell your friends and family you love them every day. Make it known so that they do not doubt your love. Joe knew that to me he was my "Old Geezer" and I know he loved me, too. After all, I can hear him saying, "Shut up! Why are you writing this book about me?"

It's because I love you, "Old Geezer".

when a joke backfires
. . .

Have you ever had something happen that turned out exactly the opposite of what you had expected? I have. I'm not sure if this chapter is going to be inspirational or not, but there was a lesson in it for me. Perhaps there will be one for someone else, as well.

One day, I was watching four of my friends play an intense game of pickleball. All four were people who had played in tournaments and won gold. It was a *very* close game. I started to root for whom I thought was the underdog, because I like to have fun and tease people I like. I wasn't mean; I thought that the normal cheering and clapping was part of the game.

At the end of the game, my underdog team beat the hardcore duo in a hard-won victory. I teased the losers and was responded to with a glare and the comment, "Don't ever say that to me again." They weren't amused.

I left the courts that day feeling confused by the interaction because it was out of the norm; teasing other players you play with all the time is *normal*. As I was driving away, I heard the Lord speak to my heart and say, "Hey, I know you didn't mean anything bad by what you said to her, but you hurt her feelings and she's not going to tell you."

I thought, *Okay, I'll go to her and apologize for that and ask her out to lunch.* Since I believed we had things in common besides pickleball, I thought it might be a good opportunity to get to know her. I didn't have her phone number, but we were connected on Facebook, so I sent her a short message saying that I was sorry and offered to take her out to lunch.

I noticed that she read the messages but didn't respond, so I waited until Monday when I was back at the courts. When I saw her I asked her if she got my apology. She snapped at me and if my head could've been bitten off, it would have been. She was so volatile that her tournament partner, who was sitting next to her, got up and walked away. We were surrounded by people and she lit into me like I have not been attacked in years.

She went on to tell me that we had nothing in common, that she'd never have lunch with me and that she didn't like me. I sat there completely stunned and crushed in spirit. It took everything in me to not cry. I apologized again for hurting her feelings and eventually got up and went for a walk to gather myself. I left early. Being verbally abused, that day, really touched a wounded part of my heart and it took some time to recoup.

But the thing that stands out to me the most about that whole interaction was that as she was berating me, the Lord spoke to my heart and told me, "It's not you she's mad it, it's Me." I heard that as clear as I hear the birds singing their songs in the morning.

I can't say that it made me feel any better, but it did explain the hostility she had toward me, in that moment. She was not a Christian, to my knowledge, so all I can surmise is that she took some anger out on me that could have been directed to someone else.

My point in sharing this is to let you know that sometimes people who are the most experienced on the court and the most intense might be the most fragile inside. That woman was hurting deeply and I didn't know why. I still don't. I do know that it is not normal to bite someone's head off for offering a sincere apology over a pickleball game.

Maybe it was just a bad day, or maybe it was a pattern in other relationships that she has. I don't know, but what I've learned in my years as a therapist is that those who bite the hardest are the often the ones who are hurting the most.

That is another life lesson learned on the pickleball court. Some people will never like you or want to be your friend; you shouldn't take it personally. How others treat you is about *them*, not *you*.

As Christians and as decent human beings, most of us have learned the golden rule: *Do unto others as you would have them do unto you.* To this day the woman in this chapter and I will occasionally play, and we're cordial on the court. She usually kills me and I'm okay with that. For me, at this point, it isn't about winning; it's about learning how to meet your foe as a friend.

That's what Jesus did for us. He loved us while we were yet sinners. He died for us.

She may never repent of her behavior or apologize for her over-reactive response, but I know God isn't done with her yet. Many years ago, I was involved in a similar scenario.

Stacy Lynn Harp. M.S.

In that case the woman stormed out of a restaurant in anger and it wasn't until we had a chance meet up about twelve years later that she admitted she was wrong and apologized.

I have hope for this player and I have seen some softness take place in subsequent months. I am praying for her and for others like her. I hope you pray for those who hurt you, too. You may never know how much it impacts them, but it will *definitely* change *you*.

the professional tournament player mindset

. . .

Earlier in this book, I addressed issues with playing with beginners and the mindset some people have when playing with people who are "not as good" as others. In this chapter I want to share what I've observed and learned from better players, and in particular those who like to play in tournaments.

I had the blessing of meeting Stephanie Lane, who is a local P.E. teacher and an awesome pickleball player. She recently won gold in the U.S. Open in 45+ Mixed Doubles with her partner Dave Weinbach. I met Stephanie on my 49th birthday because she was in my area and taking in some recreational pickleball for fun here in Spring Hill. I had no idea who she was, but she was popular! That's when I found out that she was this gold winner!

During the games I got to play with her, I was encouraged because she was a gentle instructor, when I asked for some tips. She didn't criticize me instead only offered direction and encouragement. It was like receiving an unexpected birthday present.

What stood out the most to me about Stephanie was her *joy* and *attitude*. See, attitude is *everything*. I don't care how good someone thinks they are if their attitude stinks. Negative people suck the air out of a room. We've all been there and seen that. However, the person who has some joy and enthusiasm for what they are doing will find that not only do they have more friends, but they will be successful in whatever they do. —If they have character like Stephanie Lane— they are going to excel.

I play with many overachievers and I get "instructed" by several of them—mostly men. While they mean well, I haven't asked to be taught by them. If I wanted help, I'd ask. I did ask one guy who would always get me on the serve. "What am I doing wrong?" I asked. He told me and then I knew. Does it mean that I always practice what I'm taught? No, but it *does* mean that at least I'm aware of what I need to change.

I recently played with a guy who is charming and definitely charismatic, but he's intense and demanding, as well as highly insulting. When he isn't telling me what to do on the court, he's throwing fits when he has to play with people he considers unworthy.

I find it very hurtful when another player who is more advanced than I am, treats me like a piece of dung. Yet, I have to go back and ask myself how he was treated and what kind of self-talk does he have, because if it's that bad toward me, he must have a real bully in his head.

I have learned to keep my mouth shut for the most part, because players should be *encouragers*, not *discouragers*. I would expect a better player to offer a helpful tip, not unproductive criticism. I seriously had no idea how much I would be criticized while playing. The only way I can deal with it is by reminding myself that they are either trying to make me a better player or they are just used to demeaning others to make themselves feel better.

THERE ARE ULTIMATELY two lessons I've learned from playing with the "pros". First, some of them actually want to help. They are gentle, encouraging, and have a mindset that is designed to make other players better.

Second, those who are negative and critical really have no desire to see others improve. They want to feel good about how they instruct others.

My question to those of you who are in this category is where do you tend to fall with your desire to help and how do you motive others? If the relationship is the cure and edification is the process to the cure, then is how you interact with others in line with that? Something to think about.

catching the ball and diving for shots

. . .

Are you known for something? I'm asking because if you were to survey my pickleball friends, one thing they would tell you for sure is that I am known for catching the ball. When I see the ball flying my way, I sometimes freeze in fear and just reach my hand out and *catch* it.

Other times, I can see that I am going to miss the shot. To avoid chasing the ball, I instinctively reach out and catch it.

At one point I was doing this so much that it became almost a game to see who could hit me a shot that I would catch. But here's the thing, I really didn't want to catch the ball and my friends didn't want me to, either. They began giving me suggestions.

One friend recommended that I hold my left hand behind my back, so that my hand would be behind me if I were tempted to catch the ball. Another friend, who was observing the game, actually got up and gave me a clean pink sock, telling me to put it on my hand. I actually did that until I had to serve—then I had to remove the sock.

I had other friends tell me to let the ball go by and not even *think* about catching it if I knew I couldn't get it. I had someone else advise that I hold the pickleball paddle vertically with both hands so that I could turn it quickly instead of taking my left hand out to catch the ball.

I have worked on this strategy for months and have gotten better, but it is funny that people notice when I catch the ball. Admittedly, I was a great catcher when I was a child and apparently I still have that talent.

So just like I'm a great catcher, I could list something about all my friends with whom I play regularly. Rich is probably my favorite. Rich is retired and has been one of my favorite teachers because he is someone who doesn't instruct me just to tell me what to do. He teaches without telling me "what to do". He dives for balls on the court, he puts a backspin on the ball when he serves and he's a smarty pants when it comes to his trick serve. He's a challenging opponent, and I know that going in because he's got his thing.

JR, whom I wrote about earlier in this book, is one of the best players out there. Not only does he take the time to teach new players, but he holds his own with the more advanced players. When I play against him, he teaches me how to be better because of how he treats others. He is one of the kindest and sweetest men I have ever met. He respects all players from beginner to advanced.

When I play with JR I rarely win because he's just that good, but I know when he's playing against me that he adjusts his game so I am challenged while still feeling good about myself. He's a great leader and a friend to just about everyone who will have him.

Then there's David. David is a great player but he's not someone who is out for blood. He's confident in his approach, but he's a hard player when he needs to be. He's one of my favorite teachers because he's someone who will only instruct a few times during the game in order to help someone improve. He's made me better at the net with the hard shots and lately he's been working on the lobs. In fact, David wrote the foreword to this book and he was my partner when I finally was able to get my first lob. I wrote about it on Facebook the day it happened so I will have it forever.

These are just two among dozens of others whom I love and respect. I challenge you to look where you play and whom you play with so you can see who is helping you and who is helping themselves. What their "tell" is will tell you a lot.

california pickleball vs. tennessee

. . .

Whenever I bring up the game of pickleball I usually get the question, "What is *pickleball?*" This probably should've been addressed in the first chapter of this book, but given that the target audience for this book are people of faith who play pickleball, you likely already know the answer.

One year I visited California and stayed with a close friend and tennis partner, and I had the opportunity to play pickleball in The Golden State. I was excited to teach my friend how to play and, when we found some courts and I got to teach her, it was very cool. However there were some very stark differences between California players and those in Tennessee.

Where I live in Tennessee, people are generally polite. There really is such a thing as southern hospitality. I never understood it until I moved here. The people in California were not nearly as courteous as the people in Tennessee.

That doesn't mean that they are *mean*, but they just weren't all that welcoming. Eventually I got to introduce myself and my friend Jennifer to the other players and we began. I told these California players that Jennifer was new and they didn't seem to care. That was obvious by how they tried to kill her on the court. Eventually they told us to play with other people, thereby breaking us up as a team. I wasn't against this, but I saw her fall down on another court and thought, *Seriously, why can't these people be nice?* I knew Jennifer was a great tennis player. That they were hitting the ball so hard to her that she *fell*, well, that was *not* a good thing.

I admit that I decided not to go easy when I played during the rest of our time, there. I made sure that I showed those Californians how to *really* play the game. (I am *kind* of competitive and since I grew up in California...well, I know Californians.)

So, readers, how do *you* treat others when they come to visit your pickleball court? How are you treated when you're not on your home turf? If you're like me, you probably play better when you're on a familiar court and playing with your friends, but that's not the case for everyone.

For me, the real delight during that trip was in teaching my friend Jennifer to play pickleball. She enjoyed it and we made a memory together; after all, isn't that what sports do for us? Not only are we active, but we are *making memories*.

We are building relationships and we are learning how to live in community. Community is a wonderful thing and not only builds us up in our faith, but it also helps us in our lives.

Pickleball Faith

Pickleball Faith is what this book is about. Life, relationships, the love of a game, and our faith. My radio mentor, Janet Parshall, has said numerous times, "God puts His people everywhere." Some of His people are at your job, others are at your church, and some are on the pickleball courts.

Have you ever considered this? Have you ever wondered why it is that you connect with certain people and are drawn to certain people and why you are not drawn to others? I have.

I do not think it was a mistake that God brought me to Tennessee and pickleball found me. I do not think it's a mistake you are where you are, either. There is a reason you picked up this book and decided to read it. Maybe it's because you love pickleball and maybe it's because you're a person of faith. Maybe it's because you were hoping to learn some new strategies when playing the game. Whatever the reason is, I hope that you have learned something of value and that you consider the lesson that you're being taught.

The relationship is the cure. Everyone has their own battle they are facing and for some of us, the pickleball court is our refuge. It's our sanctuary. It's our place to go so we can feel okay for a time. Never forget that.

people are more than the game
. . .

Have you ever wondered how groups of people get stereotyped? I have. We all "know" that lawyers are liars, or so we're told. Doctors "all" like to play golf. Only children are "overachievers" and the babies of any family are "salesmen". True? Not always, but these are considered stereotypes for a reason.

One thing I've learned meeting so many people on the pickleball court is that you really can't judge a book by the cover. In fact, having promoted thousands of guests over the years and having read thousands of books in my lifetime, it's true. You *can't*.

People are complex. God created us for community and recently when I was talking to a woman who came to watch her husband play, I found out that she had suffered some considerable health problems. That dear lady had been given a kidney transplant years before. That type of experience can bring fundamental changes to a person.

In fact, many of my friends have undergone some type of surgery and have stories to tell. One told me that his wife had multiple surgeries and that she fell into the two percent of the people where something went wrong. He has since avoided talking about health and discussing things like that because he'd rather not know.

I have a friend who is not yet forty, but who is going through brain surgery. Another is battling shingles and discouragement because of not being able to meet their business goals. I know another who is living in their car until they can find a new residence.

People have stories, and when I see new people who come to play pickleball, I am curious about their stories.

Why did they decide to play pickleball? Where did they hear about the game? Was it easy for them to learn? Why didn't they quit if/when they felt discouraged? Were they always good at sports? Did they play tennis or ping pong or racquetball before? Did they come from a family of athletes? Is this a sport that they believe is more individualistic or a group activity?

THERE'S SO MUCH to what we do because of who we are. Recently, I had a heart-to-heart conversation with one of my best friends about how they hurt my feelings. I admit that I have a hard time, generally speaking, when my feelings are hurt. I have a very sensitive spirit and I "feel" the rejection and I "feel" the shunning. It hurts me and yet it's an area that I'm growing in.

I was talking to one of my friends at pickleball about that very issue and she said to me, "Stacy, everyone here loves you." That really hit me. It actually made me cry, right there on the spot. Maybe because I often don't feel loved by people. I don't often feel loved for who I am. I believe that people love me for what I do for them. There's a huge difference.

I have a friend who introduced me to JJ Heller's song "What Love Really Means"

Here is the chorus:

Who will love me for me?

Not for what I have done or what I will become

Who will love me for me?

'Cause nobody has shown me what love

What love really means, what love really means

…

I will love you for you

Not for what you have done or what you will become

I will love you for you

I will give you the love

The love that you never knew

Love you for you

Not for what you have done or what you will become

I will love you for you

I will give you the love

The love that you never knew

. . .

Why do I bring this up? Because it's just a reminder that we are all fighting our own battles. Sports can be a refuge for some of us, but it may also be a place that hurts for others. Respect people where they are and remember that winning is not everything.

an angel in the
locker room

. . .

This next story is one of the most interesting things outside of the ordinary that happened at pickleball in the fall of 2018.

As I mentioned before, I host an online show called *Bible News Radio*. Through that show I have made some terrific friends and have met people literally from all over the world. One of my friends is Mia, who is a life flight paramedic and a wonderful person.

We met because she was listening to my show and wanted to have a closer walk with God. I had the opportunity to share the gospel of Jesus Christ with her and she accepted the message and received salvation! It was an amazing story. We spent a few years getting to know one another before she wanted to get baptized into her newfound faith. She drove down from Ohio and we set up a time for us to go and play pickleball, and a time for me to baptize her.

Who would've thought in a million years that pickleball and baptism would go together! God has a sense of humor.

The day Mia was baptized we spent some time in prayer before we left to play pickleball. During our prayer time, Mia and I had asked God to bless our day, to let us be able to baptize Mia in the pool at the Recreation Center (which is government facility) and to just give us a sign that He was pleased with her decision to follow Christ.

Obviously, we knew God was pleased, but we wanted a special blessing for Mia on that day.

Here's what happened. We arrived to play pickleball and enjoyed ourselves without any obstructions. After playing for a few hours, we changed our clothes so that we could get in the pool.

I strategically went up to the lifeguard who was on duty and told him that if he saw me dunking my friend into the water, not to be concerned because I was just baptizing her and there was no worry.

The lifeguard didn't seem to care what we were going to do, and I took that as a blessing from God. You may have to understand the recent hostility towards Christians in many public places these days to understand why we were concerned in the first place about these things. Our fears were abated and I was able to baptize Mia while my husband live-streamed it on Periscope (which is a now defunct live-streaming platformed owned by Twitter) so all of our friends worldwide could rejoice.

After we were done with the baptism, Mia and I returned to the locker room to change. While we were doing that, we began conversing with another lady who was there. I had never seen this other woman before. During our conversation I asked her where she was from and she replied, "Heaven."

Mia and I looked at each other and didn't say anything. I studied the lady and saw a twinkle in her eye. I seriously didn't know what to say or even *think*.

Within moments that new woman was nowhere to be found and Mia and I were standing in the locker room and wondering where she went.

"Did you hear where she said she was from? She said, 'Heaven.'"

"Who says that?"

Needless to say, we both were puzzled and excited. So we checked in with the front desk and inquired about whether or not they had seen the woman. Neither of them had and I said, "But you guys know everyone, right?"

"Yes…"

I persisted. "But you've never seen the woman we both described?"

They said, "Nope…but then again, a lot of weird things have been happening here today."

Then the four of us all started to laugh and I declared, "I believe that Mia and I were touched by an angel and that God gave us that special blessing from heaven showing that He is pleased with her decision to follow Christ."

Mia and I later went on Periscope and shared the story and the story spread through various parts of our pickleball community.

Do angels watch over us? I believe they do!

So be careful, because you may not know if you're playing with an angel.

the cupcake caregiver
. . .

What I am about to write, I'm not even sure I can share without crying.

One day when I arrived at pickleball, I discovered that one of my friends was having a birthday. This isn't uncommon as there are so many people someone is *bound* to be having a birthday on any given day.

Well, since I hadn't known before, I went through my backpack to see if I had enough change to buy some candy. Fortunately I did, so I said, "Hey, I hear it's your birthday. Happy birthday! Go get yourself a candy bar on me." He smiled, took the money, and then thanked me. I could see a tear in his eye because he was touched by my gesture. That touched me.

In fact, it always touches me when someone is emotionally moved by kindness.

That friend is Frank and he's in his seventies. He has a daughter, and he does a great deal for her. Frank is an uncomplaining man who exudes kindness and affirmation.

Pickleball Faith

Often when I was between games, I'd sit on the benches with Frank he'd ask me about my dad. Frank knows how hard it can be to be a caregiver and when I shared my struggles, he *listened*.

One day, I was running late for pickleball because I had to do something for my dad. When I was finally able to get to the courts, Frank was there and eager to see me. He said, "Hey Pancho, I have something for you." He calls me *Pancho* as a term of endearment. I love it.

I turned around to see he had a cupcake with a candle in it for me. It was my birthday and he wanted to bless me with it.

This interaction took place about a year after I gave him the money for his birthday candy.

Caregivers spend their days thinking of what is best for those they care for and forget to care for themselves. It's not often that I've had anyone go out of their way to bless me in a special way like Frank did with a cupcake.

What that taught me was that sometimes, God uses people in unexpected ways to bless you. Frank's daughter is about my age and he understands the struggles with aging. He also clearly has a father's heart and understood that he could do something kind for me that my dad couldn't do.

I saw that cupcake as a special gift from God. The Bible says that God knit me together in my mother's womb and knows the number of hairs on my head. He fearfully and wonderfully made me. That goes for you, too! The Lord knew what would touch me on that birthday and he brought to me a unique blessing from an understanding friend.

Stacy Lynn Harp. M.S.

Consider doing something nice for a fellow player. You might never know how much it means to them. And if you want to read Psalm 139 in the Bible, that is the passage that talks about how God made you in your mother's womb. It's one of my favorite passages.

pickleball during a pandemic
. . .

If someone had told me that the world would be changed the way it was in 2020, I would not have believed it.

This book has taken a few years to put together and when I first started it we had open play with pickleball. Then in early 2020, COVID-19 hit and everything was put on hold —including pickleball.

It was a huge adjustment for all of us diehard players who loved to hang out at the courts with our friends.

It certainly was for me. I set up a bowl in my living room and would practice hitting a pickleball across my living room to see if I could get the ball into the bowl. Exciting right? Not so much. It was rather awful.

Some of my friends initially went into our pickleball Facebook group to share what they were doing but all *that* did was make me long to hit the courts.

Eventually though, we were able to go back to the recreation center and play under "new rules". Frankly, I wasn't thrilled with the new rules and no one else was either, but at least we got to play.

The new rules consisted of having our temperature taken every time we wanted to play. We had to wear a face mask while we were in the building, which was ridiculous because we could walk down the hall with the mask and then take it off once we were with our other players.

There was no more open play. *This* is what was the hardest for most people, because when you're used to showing up to play with whoever else showed up, now we were forced to figure out not only *how* to get in touch with others in our group, but it severely limited *whom* you could reach out to and play with.

I had an advantage of having phone numbers and connections within our group due to the t-shirt sale I mentioned in this book before. I became one of the connectors in our community.

This taught me a lot about the person I had become while playing in the pickleball community.

Another thing the pandemic did for me was to make me aware of whom I could call a *friend*. Someone I could reach out to and ask, "Hey, wanna play on Tuesday?"

I know it may sound odd, but for me, this was a big deal. I actually feel vulnerable writing this because when I first started playing this game I really didn't have any friends in this area. Pickleball became, for me, a refuge from my other daily activities. It wasn't work related. It wasn't ministry-focused as my normal job was. It was simply a thing to do for *fun*.

Once the pandemic arrived, I had to figure out whom to play with, and so did many other people.

What I noticed happening was that the better players ended up playing together nearly exclusively, while the rest of us tried to figure out whom we could *all* play with. I ended up connecting with about six friends with whom I regularly rotated games and that became our new routine.

Another new development was that we didn't have to *wait* to play games any longer! At first this was tough because none of us were used to playing for almost two hours without a break, but eventually we all built our stamina up and it became our "new normal".

And as is the case with many "new normals", sometimes that got a little bit tiring, at least for me.

I see one of the joys of the game as playing with many different folks. But during the pandemic, most of us had to just keep playing with the same people or we didn't play at all. I found that for me, while I enjoyed playing, it was hard when your games weren't as challenging as they could be with a greater variety of players.

I noticed that as time went on, due to the familiarity of the group I was playing with, that me and another friend started to feel frustrated with not being challenged as much. I knew I needed to be more challenged and my friend did too. However, neither of us felt completely comfortable going outside of our group. At first, that is.

WHEN I STARTED to find myself feeling resentful that I was having to play with someone I didn't want to play with all the time, I had to examine my heart and consider my motives. As a Christian, I take my faith seriously and even in that, God was at work.

I had to learn to set boundaries, even if no one else knew what they were. I believe that in order to have a healthy relationships, you have to have a healthy relationship with yourself first, and a significant part of that is establishing boundaries.

How do you consider someone more highly than yourself? Was I becoming codependent on the people with whom I played? Was it *okay* for me to want to play with others who challenged me more? Why did I feel bad even thinking I couldn't have the right to not play with someone I wasn't having as much fun with?

My fear in even writing about this is that people may think I'm selfish, but the struggle I'm trying to explain is that I was trying to find the balance between not being selfish while trying to meet my own personal needs.

Another friend of mine was struggling with the same issue. He felt like I did: he wanted to play the game but he wasn't thrilled with playing with some of the same people who were not as good as he was. Yet, being the nice person he was, he opted to play even when the others would criticize him. That really got to me.

Then it occurred to me that one of the biggest differences between what I have dubbed "elite" players and the more "regular" folk is that the elite players had no problem saying, "Hey, you aren't at my level and you're going to hurt my game." I understand that perspective, because when you're a tournament player, you can't afford to play down. But when you're not a tournament player and all you want to do is play, well, is it right to only want to play with those people you *want* to play with?

I had to come to the conclusion that the answer is yes. It all comes down to attitude, that's why.

So even in a pandemic where the world was turned upside down, God was working in my heart and mind regarding *attitude*.

The other thing God was showing me during this time had to do with *leadership*. John Maxwell is famous for saying that "Leadership is influence," and during this time I realized that God was calling me to step into the role of a leader in order to connect other players.

At first I thought it was cool. I felt special, because I had all the phone numbers and contacts, but eventually it started to humor me more than anything.

I felt amused because I didn't really understand why people didn't maintain the connections themselves once they were established. Rather than getting in touch with one another on their own, they would defer to me to make the connections every week.

That actually started to become annoying because I kept thinking to myself, "Why don't they just exchange phone numbers and ask each other to play? They don't need me for this."

And again, I found the Lord trying to show me more about attitudes and leadership. I learned that leadership wasn't just influence, but leadership was also the ability to delegate. So I finally learned to say what I was thinking and to hand off the responsibility to others in the group. Once I learned to do that, I found that more people got to play and less stress seemed to be had by all.

Pickleball Faith is really all about growing in those relationships and learning to communicate well with others and ourselves. It's about hearing the voice of God in our lives and making His love known, even in the oddest of circumstances.

I know for me, I am blessed to have the friends that I have and I know that pretty much any day of the week I want to play, I can pick up the phone and text a dozen people and find a few more who will come. That's a pretty cool thing.

pickleball faith

. . .

As I've thought about how to wrap up this book and the lessons that I've learned, one thought I had to share concerns priorities.

I stated in the beginning of the book that *the relationship is the cure*. I feel a need to end this book by emphasizing *priorities in life*.

As an entrepreneur who is very serious about my business I am around many people who are involved in the world of personal development. Some engage in personal development by reading books like this one. Others may sign up for a seminar, listen to a podcast, go on a retreat, hire a coach and so on.

In life, if you want to go far and succeed at anything you have to first figure out what it is and, second, learn to make it a priority.

I chose to make pickleball a priority in my life and I am so thankful I did. However, I would be remiss if, after bearing my soul in this book, I did not share with you why Jesus is my *first* priority. Without my relationship with Jesus Christ, I would not have even considered writing this book in the first place. *Pickleball Faith* wouldn't be called *Pickleball Faith*, it would be called something like *Pickleball: Why I Love It* or *Pickleball: How to Make Friends and Enemies*. I'm kind of kidding about the enemies part, but I think you get my point.

Recently a long-time Facebook friend offered something on her page that caught my attention. She tagged me in a post about joining a group having to do with daily Bible reading for fifty days with other people. In essence it was an accountability group for people who struggle with reading their Bibles every day.

My first thought was that I was touched that I was considered for the opportunity and my second thought was that I didn't need any help with my Bible reading. After all, I'm the host of *Bible News Radio* and I read the Bible every day. I open up my You Version app and see the verse of the day, I read it and sometimes I even post the graphic on my Facebook page. Additionally, I know enough scripture to make it work when I talk about current events and I didn't really need the help.

However, as the Lord often does, He gave me that opportunity as a gift and I accepted the invitation from my friend and began a fifty-day journey with about twelve other people whom I did not know.

The way this group was set up is that we would meet every morning at 7:30 on Zoom and then we would check in and tell the leader, Pam Gillaspie, (who is also a pickleball player) where we were going to read in the Bible for the next 30 minutes. Then we would all shut off our Zoom cameras, mute our mics, and read. Pam would come back when the time was up and ask who would like to share something about what they had just read.

I found this very fascinating because I love to hear about what people think about God and I knew I was going to get a first hand look at how God was working in these people's lives. And, well, I was right. But then something amazing happened. After a few weeks our group had started to bond, and God started to reveal in me areas that I needed to deal with.

The people in this group listened to me, they prayed with me and they encouraged me in my daily walk with God.

I WEPT and confessed some of my sin and error in thinking and no one judged me. They just loved me where I was. It was healing for me because the people in the group were truly offering the love of Jesus as I was dealing with the stuff God was showing me.

I went into those first meetings with some spiritual pride and thinking I didn't need what Pam was offering. Within months, I was on a mission to tell others about how God moved in my life, due to being a part of a community with daily involvement in His word.

There are lies in the world that say you can be the master of your own destiny and being a lone ranger is a good thing. You cannot do life alone. God never intended for any of us to go through life alone.

In fact, when God created Adam in the garden and set him up with just the animals at first, Adam wasn't content. So God created Eve and gave him a companion. I will keep to the main point here, which is this: God told Adam and Eve to procreate and they did and you and I are here because of that. God made family and community was born.

I had to make my time with the Lord a *priority*. I thought I had been because of the actions that I mentioned above. However, the reality was that I was exercising what I would call a lazy faith. I, like many believers, found a verse of the Bible and made it say what I wanted and went on my way. I was ignoring the love letter that God gave me and ignoring the whole message surrounding those verses. Context is everything.

How could I even think God was all right with that I seriously had to consider that question. I would never read a newspaper article and take a quote out of context and apply that to my life, and yet with the Bible, that was what I was doing. My priorities were out of order and God made sure I knew I needed to make a change.

God knew that I needed to return to Him, my first love. He knew how to get my attention because you see, I was a wounded and hurting person. I had some painful church experiences and essentially left the community and fellowship, even though I never lost my faith and continued to live my life the best I could for Him.

Spiritually, I was severely crippled and didn't even know it. I had cut myself off from the lifeblood of community with the body of Christ and so I was basically stuck. My spiritual life was stagnant.

My priority had been *what I wanted*. I wanted to feel comfortable. I wanted to be alone. I didn't want to share where I really was, because I believed that no one cared and people just wanted to use me.

On some level I was bitter, unforgiving, and had turned into a relatively judgmental person. Even as I am writing this, I'm feeling quite vulnerable. Honestly, even though I might not have been walking around yelling at people and condemning them outwardly, in my *heart* I have been pretty critical and the Bible says that out of the abundance of the heart, the mouth speaks.

Now, if you're beginning to think, "Would you get on with the point here? I'm beginning to feel like you're preaching at me," just hang in there with me. I'm being vulnerable and it's not easy.

There's an old adage that says, "Hurt people, hurt people." I have no clue who said it, but it's well known in some circles. A few years ago, however, a friend of mine quoted someone as saying, "Hurt people *who are not heard*, hurt people." That added another layer.

If you've been hurt by someone and continue to walk around without dealing with that pain, then you're not likely making progress in life. If you've tried to share your pain with others and haven't been heard, it's easy to carry that feeling onward.

However, if you take the time to risk sharing your hurt and *are* heard, that can change everything for you.

One of the best gifts in life is the ability to hear someone else. One of the worst things in life is to be ignored and completely invalidated. That is why, for me, writing this book has been so important.

I grew up in an environment with people who ignored my hurt, created pain for me and did everything they could to crush and break me as a person. The level of rejection I have had to overcome has been massive. How I have done that and how long it took, is another whole book in itself, but I will say for now, that if you find a great therapist and are committed to the journey, that with God can change your life. It has mine.

My husband recently summed those experiences up by reminding me that when a tree grows there are rings that form within the trunk of the tree. Whatever impact those rings had in the beginning are deeply rooted and never leave the tree, but are a part of the tree. Childhood trauma is part of that for me. Maybe it is for you, too.

If it's not childhood trauma that impacts you, maybe you had some type of trauma as an adult. I know many people who have endured divorce or addiction issues. There are other issues like bankruptcy or infertility that are impactful. Issues and the pain they bring can feel endless.

My hope in sharing part of my journey with you and sharing the unfolding thoughts and behaviors that have led to self-awareness, is that you, reader, will see how God has worked in my life. Maybe you can reflect on the ideas of connection and community, and see how it is that you function among others.

How do you think others see you? Have you ever asked them? How do you see yourself? Is it evident in what your thoughts communicate to you? Are you someone who has an encouraging word for others or are you someone who always has to correct or condemn?

These are important issues and they play out in community, no matter what type of community it is. It may be with your friends playing pickleball or it could be in your church fellowship. Your community is clear in those who surround you.

Pickleball Faith

I am going to wrap up—really!—with another thing God has shown me. For almost eighteen years I have hosted my online radio show *Bible News Radio* and built an online community of believers who respect and bless what my husband and I do. I have a Facebook group called Daily Disciples that I established in order to minister to people in the group so that they would be encouraged by reading in the Bible every day.

MY PROBLEM with that group was that no one would *engage*. It did not matter what I did, how many encouraging videos I put up, how many quotes or songs from YouTube—no one would engage. At first I blamed it on Facebook liking to hide content, but after awhile I decided to actually ask the Lord. Novel idea, right?

Well, after spending time in prayer, I got the thought that maybe I should ask people if they would like to read from the Bible in the group. My first thought after that was, "Yeah right, Lord. No one is going to do that. Are you kidding me?"

But then I thought, *Why not give it a try?* I had nothing to lose. If no one wanted to read for the group, I was no worse off. If people decided to read, it would be fun to watch.

So, in faith and with high skepticism, I shot a text message to my list and then posed it to the group and— literally within minutes—I had eight people who said they would love to try to do a daily Bible reading in the group.

What took me off guard was *who* came forward. Seriously, I was floored, because the people who responded and said they would like to try were people I personally would never had considered to ask to read.

Why? Well, because of my preconceived ideas and whom I thought they were.

For example, one of the women who came forward is a lady who is legally blind. She reads slowly and with a magnifying glass. Her husband, who didn't read the Bible before this, saw her reading and he wanted to join in.

Another person has a large family asked if she could read and so I said yes, why not. Who am I to not let her read? A few times since she began, her husband has also joined in with her.

I could tell you stories about each of the other readers, and how what I thought was wrong about each one of them. Not because I was judging them all negatively, but because I did not *know* them.

God began to speak to me through all of my friends and I received love, support, prayer for my family, and—most of all—encouragement to continue to go and thrive in my faith.

All of that happened because of *community*. As in our pickleball community where we have bonds and connections among those we play with, we all have a backstory that others do not know, unless they ask.

My hope and prayer is that as you grow as a pickleball player with your dinking and banging, that you grow even more as a person and always remember that the relationship we have with one another is the cure and the relationship you can have with the Lord was paid for by His grace and merciful death on the cross for your sin.

John 3:16 - 17 says:

For God so loved the world, that He gave His only begotten Son, that whoever believes in Him shall not perish, but have eternal life. 17"For God did not send the Son into the world to judge the world, but that the world might be saved through Him.

Jesus died to save you from your sin. He didn't come into the world to condemn you. So, know that if you've been hurt in the church or by church people, it's not God's fault. He loves you. He wants to know you personally and all you have to do is ask.

Romans 10:13 says:

for "WHOEVER WILL CALL ON THE NAME OF THE LORD WILL BE SAVED."

THAT IS my desire and that is His desire. We all have faith in something and someone at some point in our lives. I have laid out my faith in a book about pickleball and how God has taught me life lessons. An even greater book is the Holy Bible which is where you can learn about the ultimate way to have faith and you can learn to live, love, and walk in faith with Jesus. That is my hope and prayer for you.

That and that you stay behind the kitchen line and enjoy the new bounce serve!

afterword

Since the time I began this book around 2019 many things have happened in the world of pickleball. I had mentioned taking care of my father in the beginning of the book and that had taken much of my time. Sadly, in January of 2021, my father, Clayton Perrotte, died and is now at home with the Lord.

My pickleball community of friends surrounded me with love, prayers, and listening ears and hearts when my dad died. I will always treasure the day my father came to watch me play pickleball and the community thanked my father for his service in the Korean War. There are many retired veterans who play pickleball and they showed respect for my dad.

The other major thing that has happened since I wrote this book is that now pickleball is back to open play and pickleball has exploded on the national scene. My friends and I are enjoying more hours to play with each other and yet at the same time, if we desire to play with certain people, we can now reserve a court too! So something good came

Afterword

from the pandemic playing rules and I think it's a win for everyone.

Pickleball has also become more mainstream since I started writing this book. Bill Gates and Brené Brown and other famous people have been in the media talking about how they play pickleball. Recently, Brené Brown even shared about her own experience playing the sport and how she didn't play well at first, but then she was able to snap out of her poor serving streak and eventually play and win the games she was in. She shared that one of the things she feared was that someone was going to videotape her playing horribly and then post it all over social media and then she would be a laughing stock. I thought this was fascinating, coming from a researcher who specializes in writing about vulnerability. Dr. Brené Brown is someone I enjoy learning from and who understands how people can choose to treat each other and why it matters even in through pickleball.

Other celebrities that play pickleball include Ellen Degeneres, Jenna Bush Hager, Kim Kardashian, Jillian Michaels, Gary Vaynerchuk, Andre Kirk Agassi, Dr. Phil and—believe it or not—many of the Chicago Cubs baseball players have taken up the game.

resources

The following resources are places you can go to learn to play pickleball, get involved in a tournament or grow in your faith! Enjoy!

USA Pickleball
https://usapickleball.org/
Pickleball Tournaments
https://www.pickleballtournaments.com/
Professional Pickleball Registry
https://pprpickleball.org/
Pickleball Faith
https://www.pickleballfaith.com
Heart Tug International
https://www.hearttug.org

about stacy lynn harp

Stacy Lynn can be reached by email at stacylynn@hearttug.org

She holds an M.S. degree in Clinical Psychology, with many years spent counseling women, children and couples in a variety of circumstances, and always from a biblical perspective. She is also the Founder of Heart Tug International and host of Bible News Radio. She has been married to her husband Randall since 1992 and lives in beautiful Middle, Tennessee.

Stacy Lynn loves pickleball, her lovable fur babies, rocky road ice cream and cardinals. When she is not playing pickleball with her Pro Kennex Kinetic paddle, she's leading bible studies and encouraging others in their faith and writing other books.

Her first book **Five Successful Ways to Stay Depressed** is a comical, very *short* book addressing the issue of depression and can be found on Amazon.

Heart Tug International
5016 Spedale Court #249
Spring Hill, TN 37174

Made in the USA
Monee, IL
10 June 2022

97811139R00059